Team Building for Managers

90 Minute Guides

Michelle N. Halsey

Silver City Publications & Training, L.L.C.
P.O. Box 1914
Nampa, ID 83653
https://www.silvercitypublications.com/shop/

ISBN-10: 1-64004-036-6
ISBN-13: 978-1-64004-036-6

Contents

Chapter 1 – Team Building Benefits

Your organization's people are its greatest asset, and when they work together as a team they accomplish even more. But teamwork doesn't just happen. Teams have to be created, developed, and continuously nurtured. A solid team building strategy can create an environment of greater collaboration and collegiality, which is good not only for the bottom line for your people themselves. There are many different ways to build a team, and to continue fostering a sense of teamwork. Developing a diverse team building tool kit helps your people grow at every stage.

At the end of this tutorial, you should be able to:

- Discuss the benefits of team work

- Understand the importance of intentionally fostering teamwork

- Determine strategies your organization can take to build teams

- Understand the benefits of games and social activities in building a team

- Apply the principles of team building to your own organization

What Are the Benefits of Team Building?

Team building has many benefits, to both the organization and the individual employees that make up the tam. Team building helps to create a sense of cohesion, reinforce shared goals and values, and greater camaraderie. Team building also helps teams be more effective, as they communicate more openly and are more motivated to pursue shared goals. An investment in team building activities is an investment in success.

Better Communication and Conflict Resolution

One of the greatest benefits of team building is better communication. People who have a sense that they are on a team, with shared values and goals, are more likely to be personally invested in one another. This facilitates communication because people want to reach shared goals, and have a shared sense of purpose or vision. Team building helps team members develop strong communication skills, and also helps the team establish communication systems. Improved conflict resolution is another benefit of team building. Clearer communication in and of itself helps to facilitate better conflict resolution. The shared goals and values of a team, along with the increased personal investment and stronger personal relationships that form in a team, also helps to foster an environment in which conflicts are addressed openly and productively.

Effectiveness

Team building helps to create more effective teams. Team building activities create a sense that team members are pulling together toward a common goal or set of goals. This sense of shared purpose tends to foster effectiveness and productivity. Team building also helps the team find greater effectiveness through developing skills in delegating tasks, collaborating, communicating, and creating processes that leverage each team member's skills. A team that has a sense that they are working together, and in which the team members trust each other to honor their commitments, works more efficiently and effectively.

Motivation

Team building activities can be a powerful source of motivation. Spending time together as a team is a chance to reinforce shared goals, set new shared goals, and strengthen relationships with team members. A sense of shared goals and values serves as valuable motivation. When infused with a spirit of healthy competition and camaraderie, team building activities also motivate team members because there is a sense of not just working for one's self but for the good of the entire team. Team building activities help remind your team what they're working for and why, which can be a valuable boost to motivation.

Camaraderie

One of the most powerful benefits of team building is a sense of camaraderie. The reinforcement of shared values and shared goals which goes along with team building helps create a sense of camaraderie and collegiality. Team building activities help to strengthen the interpersonal relationships between team members.

Team building gives team members a chance to get to know each other beyond just their work functions, and helps to foster a sense of shared identity. Taking the time to create relationships that go beyond simply interacting over work responsibilities helps team members to invest more in each other emotionally and personally. This creates a sense that team members aren't just pieces of a process, but people with feelings and needs. When team members have a sense of camaraderie, they are more likely to want to collaborate, help each other, and support each other.

Chapter 2 – Types of Team Building Activities

There is a wide variety of team building activities that you can use in developing your team. Using a mix of games, activities, and social events helps keep your team building plan interesting and engaging. Each team will respond to different activities, so be open to switching up the type of team building you do. Also seek input from your team about which activities they enjoy and find valuable.

Games

Studies show that fostering a sense of play is a great way to foster camaraderie and team work. Using games also infuses a sense of fun and, depending on the game, a sense of friendly competition that can help people open up and form strong relationships. There are a variety of types of games you can use in team building, including:

- Icebreakers or "get to know you" games

- Shared task games

- Problem-solving games

- Interaction games

No matter what type of game or games you chose for a team building session, there are several key components to any effective team building game:

- Focus on learning and remembering names

- Focus on the game itself

- Focus on strengthening relationships

- Cheers and pats on the back

Activities

Group activities can also be a great way to build a team. Activities that are created specifically for team building are one option. Your training department can be a great source of information for team building activities, and there are a variety of excellent books and workbooks to draw from. Activities which are not specifically "team building" activities, but which encourage your team to interact with each other, are also valuable for building your team. Simply engaging in an activity together, whether a recreational activity or a community service activity, can give your team members a chance to take the focus off of work and instead focus on getting to know each other.

Education

Training, development, and education also offer opportunities for team building. When your team builds a new skill together, learns a new technology or process, or otherwise engages in professional development as a group, this reinforces shared goals. Include some education in your training plan about team building specifically as well. Engaging in education about how to function better as a team has clear benefits, as team members build a set of skills together that they can then apply to working with each other. However, any shared learning experience has the potential to create a stronger team. When people learn together, they support each other's development and can find a shared sense of purpose in learning something new or building a new skill. Take time to ask your team what they'd like to learn. You can also focus on the team's strengths and development areas in planning education.

Social Gatherings

Don't underestimate the power of social gatherings to build your team. While it's always important to recognize that family and other commitments can make it difficult for some team members to engage in social time outside of work, gatherings can still be a valuable tool in your team building kit. Whether you have regular team lunches where the topic of conversation is anything but work, an annual holiday gathering, or period get together after work for dinner, drinks, or other fun, social gatherings help to take your team out of their work environment so they can focus on each other. Ask your team what type of gatherings they would enjoy. Be wary of gatherings that center on alcohol, both for liability reasons and because it excludes those team members who do not drink. Vary the type of social gatherings so that those who may not enjoy one type of gathering have other options. Encouraging your team to spend time together as colleagues helps to further foster camaraderie and relationships.

Chapter 3 – Games

Many studies show that we learn best through play, and that dedicated play time is vital for our mental and emotional health. Games offer a way to bring an element of play to the workday. Games are also a way to help break down barriers by adding a spark of fun. In addition, games require us to think creatively, problem-solve, and work together. All these, plus the bonding element of shared laughter, are valuable for team building.

Games for Introductions

A great place to insert a game into your team building is during introductions. Often called "ice breakers," these games encourage people to think creatively about themselves, and offer their team members a chance to get to know them in a new way. Ice breakers help people get to know others not just by name, but by their interests, experiences, and memories. Ice breaker can be serious or humorous, and can sometimes serve as a launching point for other activities. There are many excellent books and websites with ice breakers out there, so take the time to choose a few you can use. Using different ice breakers means that people can "get to know" even people they have worked with for a long time! Some ideas for ice breakers:

- Three Truths and a Lie: Have each person tell three truths and one lie about him/herself. Then have others see if they can guess the lie

- My Favorite: After introducing themselves, have each member give their favorite of something – candy, music, song, color. "I'm Jane, and my favorite candy bar is Snickers."

- Sort and Mingle: "Sort" team members into groups by category (birth month, for example). Have them get to know each other. Then have them "mingle" with other groups.

Games to Build Camaraderie

Games are a great way to build camaraderie and add an element of play to work. The element of friendly competition helps team members to bond and reinforces shared values and goals. They key when using a game to foster camaraderie is to find a game that includes everyone. Hierarchies in the team (if they exist) should be erased for the game, so that everyone is participating as equals. The focus of the game should be working together and bonding, rather than simply winning. However, having a prize or other reward for the "winners" is also a nice way to foster health competition and collaboration. Some games that can be used to build camaraderie include:

- Scavenger hunts

- Puzzles

- Timed challenges

- Binder clip tag and other "Office Olympics "games

Games for Problem-Solving

Games that center on problem-solving are a fabulous tool for team building. When you give a team a problem to solve, and then add an element of fun, you encourage everyone to work together towards a shard goal. Some of the games that are good for building camaraderie also focus on problem-solving, because working together to solve a problem is an excellent way for people to bond. Scavenger hunts, treasure hunts, and puzzles offer a chance to solve problems while also building a sense of camaraderie. You can choose a "real life" problem as the focus of your game, or you can give your team a somewhat silly challenge that requires them to use critical thinking, creative thinking, and problem-solving skills. Word games are an excellent choice for problem-solving. Hands-on challenges help to promote problem-solving while also giving rich chances for laughter and interaction.

Games to Stimulate Interaction

Another way that games can help build teams is in stimulating interaction. Some of the ice breaker games can be adapted to stimulate interaction rather than just introduce people to one another. Games that require team members to work together also stimulate interaction in a way that regular work duties do not. Even better are games where team members must interact with many people as part of the game – the Sort and Mingle, for example. Games that stimulate interaction may give people on a team who don't interact much beyond the necessities a chance to interact in new ways. It's also useful, when using interaction games, to focus on getting people to interact with others outside their normal circle. When people are "forced" to interact, they often find that they have much in common with people they might not have sought out.

Chapter 4 – More Team Building Games

Never underestimate the power of play as you build your team. Games can be used to break the ice, to stimulate interaction, and to focus people on common goals. Games also add an element of levity and fun to work relationships, which can make it easier for people to interact and find camaraderie. Games can also be used to foster trust, motivate your team, build communication, and help strengthen conflict resolution skills.

Games to Build Trust

When many people hear "trust building games," they think of the classic game from high school theater where one person falls back and trusts the others to catch them. And while such games do build trust, there are other ways playing games together can help build your people's confidence in each other. Games that build trust are useful in helping your team build confidence in each other and in themselves. By allowing your team to take risks in carefully controlled environments like trust-building games, you empower them to feel safer taking risks and trusting each other on the job. Some trust-building games to try include:

- **Mine Field:** A course of "mines" is laid out (with cups, cones, etc.). Then one person is blindfolded and guided through the maze by a team mate's spoken directions.

- **Eye Contact:** Have each team member make eye contact with a partner for 50 seconds without looking away.

- **Willow in the Wind:** The old classic! Have one team member stand in a circle of colleagues, then let the others push and roll him or her around the circle, trusting they will not let him or her fall.

Games to Motivate

Games can be a great way to motivate your team. Studies show that healthy competition can motivate teams toward goals. When using a game to motivate your team, find a way to incorporate skills they use (or should be using) on the job into the game. Learning to use these skills to win a game can be a powerful motivator to use them in the daily job. You can also use these games as part of training on new skills and procedures, as a way to make learning fun and engaged. As with many of the other types of games, there is overlap – a motivational game may also build communication and conflict resolution, stimulate interaction, or promote camaraderie. Practicing skills in the relative low-stakes environment of a game helps your people be less afraid to make mistakes and take risks, which will make them more comfortable using the new skills in actual situations.

Games to Build Communication

Communication-building games are a worthwhile investment. Games that build communication can also help to build trust and promote interaction, as well as building a sense of camaraderie. Games also give your team low-risk ways to try new communication strategies that they can use in real life situations on the job. Finding games that require your team members to communicate in order to solve a problem, navigate an obstacle, or otherwise "win" gives you a chance to see how they work together (or don't) and how they communicate (or don't) in real time. Some communications games to try:

- **The Human Knot:** Have 6-8 people stand in a tight knot. Have them take hands. Now tell them to untie the knot and form a circle without letting go of hands. They must communicate how to get untangled.

- **Listen to Me!** Discuss traits of good and bad listeners. Then have team members get into pairs. While one team member talks, the other plays the role of "bad listener." Then have the listener play the role of "good listener." Switch roles. Then reflect.

- **Make a Team With...:** Similar to the Sort and Mingle, in this exercise team members have to build a team quickly depending on a characteristic you call out – shoe type, hair color, etc. This shows different ways to quickly communicate and form teams.

Games for Conflict Resolution

Like games for communication, games for conflict resolution offer a chance to try out skills in a low-risk environment. Finding creative ways to solve a conflict or problem is a valuable skill, and using games is a fun and low-stress way to explore it. Having your team work on conflict resolution skills in a game setting helps them feel comfortable enough with those skills that they are able to apply them in real-life conflicts later. Many games that are used to build communication skills generally can be used to build conflict resolution and negotiation games. Some idea for conflict resolution games include:

- **Advocacy and Inquiry:** Have team members experiment with different ways of acting in conflict situations. Then discuss how they might handle the situation more effectively.

- **Like a Dog With a Bone:** Have each person write down a workplace conflict involving them which is unresolved. Place the papers in a bowl – these are the "bones." Then pick bones from the bowl and discuss as a group how the situation can be resolved.

- **I Statements:** Practice using "I statements" as a way to resolve conflict productively.

Chapter 5 – Activities

Sharing activities is another way to build teams. Team building activities sometimes get a bad rap as boring, cheesy, or pointless. However, well-constructed team building activities can bring many benefits – better communication, better camaraderie, greater exchange of ideas. Finding activities that engage your team is a great way to build skills, create an atmosphere of collaboration, and create a stronger team overall.

Activities to Build Camaraderie

Sharing in an activity together builds camaraderie among your team members. The sense of having a shared experience can be a powerful way to form bonds and encourage team members to build relationships. Infusing activities with a sense of fun and play also encourages laughter and camaraderie among your people. Whether you choose to use activities that have many of the features of games, or find activities that are more focused on building relationships and skills for your team, the benefits in enhanced relationships, which brings a host of other benefits. When choosing activities that build camaraderie, focus on activities in which people participate as equals, and in which everyone can participate. One strategy is to break your team up into smaller groups, which allows for more one on one interaction. Some activities to consider as you build camaraderie on your team:

- **Building Challenges:** Teams build a product – bikes are a popular option – that will be donated to charity.

- **Charity Drive:** Teams collect for an agreed-upon charity. Food pantries or toy drives are common choices.

- **Office Olympics:** Teams compete in a variety of office-themed events, with fun prizes

Activities for Idea Sharing

The most successful teams share ideas. Hopefully your team shares their ideas in the course of their regular work. Activities that focus on sharing ideas can help team members get more comfortable speaking up about their ideas, and with hearing the ideas of others. Activities that focus on sharing ideas can also do much to build communication skills and camaraderie. When you encourage your people to really listen to each other when they speak, they are learning more than just the specific ideas that are surfaced. They are reinforcing good listening skills, which are invaluable. Some ideas for activities for sharing ideas include:

- **Graffiti:** Place poster boards or flipboards around the room with a concept listed at the top of each one. Have team members circulate and write words the associate with the concept on the board. Then discuss.

- **Brainstorm:** Generate ideas as a group to solve a problem, plan an activity, or otherwise use shared ideas. Have someone write these on a flipboard. Use a ball or other item to make sure each person gets to speak.

- **Think, Pair, Share:** Give the team time to think over an idea. Then have them pair up to discuss ideas. Finally, bring the whole group back together to share what they came up with.

Activities to Build Trust

Much like trust-building games, trust-building activities help your team develop confidence in themselves and others. Activities designed to build trust help your team members take calculated risks in a relatively safe, supportive environment. This can help them feel more empowered and confident to take those risks outside the activity session as well. Sharing in an activity where one has to take a risk and succeeds not only builds trust in his or her team mates, but helps to build camaraderie. Having shared in an activity in which they were vulnerable together changes people's relationships, and typically makes them more willing to trust each other and be vulnerable in other instances. In addition to the trust-building games mentioned earlier, some popular trust-building activities include:

- Obstacle courses

- Bungee jumping

- Ropes courses

- Parasailing

- Active listening

- Boundary breaking

Activities to Stimulate Interaction

Most activities you might choose for your team will stimulate some level of interaction. However, you can choose activities which are specifically geared to generate interaction as well. These activities encourage people to get to know each other in a new way, share ideas, and collaborate or cooperate. Techniques such as the Sort and Mingle and Think, Pair, Share are excellent ways to stimulate interaction among your team. You may also choose to engage in activities such as volunteering, participating in a community event, or engaging in an event such as a scavenger hunt. The goal is to get your team interacting in ways that transcend their workday interactions, so that they get to know each other and expand their understanding of one another. When people interact outside a task-oriented context, it helps to round out their relationship and may give people a chance to interact meaningfully with people they have little contact with in a work setting.

Chapter 6 – More Team Building Activities

Activities go a long way toward building a strong, cohesive team. Activities are chances to build and practice skills, strengthen relationships, and interact on a deeper level. Team activities give members shared experiences, which they draw on in creating a team identity. Activities can also be used to motivate your team, improve team work, strengthen communication and conflict resolution, and generally create a greater sense of unity.

Activities to Motivate

Activities can serve as a great motivation. One way to use activities to motivate is to use them as a reward, though this is not the only way. Engaging in shared activities in which they learn new skills, contribute to the organization or community, and otherwise stretch themselves and their abilities can be a powerful motivating force for a team. You can also use activities to help team members – and the team as a whole – discover their motivators. Getting clear on what motivates your people and your team makes it easier to offer appropriate rewards and motivators. Almost any activity can be used to generate motivation.

Activities to Improve Working Together

Activities are an excellent tool for improving cooperation, collaboration, and other aspects of working together. Activities such as building challenges or cooperative games and sports are ideal for focusing on the way a team works together. When a team has to create a product, navigate an obstacle, or complete a puzzle as a group, they employ skills in communication, collaboration, negotiation, and more. Working together in an activity also adds a level of fun and take some of the pressure off as well. When teams can polish their skills in working together in a fun, supportive, low-stakes environment such as a group activity, they are better able to see what they do well and what needs work. They can then take this and apply it to real work situations.

Activities to Build Communication

Activities also offer a chance for team members to build communications. Games and formal training scenarios can help communication, but may feel artificial. Engaging in group activities, whether it's a team sport or organizing a charity drive, requires that team members communicate. Because activities are generally lower risk than work deliverables, they give the team a chance to experiment with new communication strategies. Team members may also work with colleagues in activities that they don't interact with regularly in their work duties, so activities offer chances to communicate with a variety of different people. Activities may also offer a chance to communicate in different ways than team member's everyday tasks require, which gives them a chance to try out new skills.

Activities for Conflict Resolution

Activities offer a great setting for conflict resolution and negotiation. This is true of activities specifically designed to simulate workplace conflicts and allow team members to work on conflict skills. However, it is also true of activities in which people must work together more generally. Conflicts and the need for negotiation arise when people must communicate and cooperate. Team activities offer an environment where team members can try out conflict resolution and negotiation skills. And because activities take place in an environment which is supportive and collegial, people may feel safer trying out negotiation and conflict resolution skills here than they would in conflicts that arise on the job. Studies show that one of the benefits of team activities, whether sports or theater or any other group activity, for children is improved ability to negotiate and resolve conflict. This holds true for the adults on your team, too! Activities allow people a chance to work things out on their own, try out different ways of negotiating and solving conflict, and experiencing how others do these things as well.

Chapter 7 – Social Gatherings

Social gatherings are another way to build your team. Always be mindful that social gathering outside of work hours might be difficult for some of your team members, especially those who have family obligations or who have long commutes. However, finding ways for your team to socialize together can help build relationships and create camaraderie that is difficult to achieve in a structured work setting. Use a variety of social gatherings, timed at different times, to encourage your team to socialize together.

Singing/Karaoke

Nearly everyone loves to sing. Singing or karaoke can be a great activity to help your team have fun and grow closer. Whether you go to a karaoke spot in your city, or bring a karaoke machine into the office, this is a fun way for everyone to take a little risk and be creative with their colleagues. Encourage everyone to participate, stressing that the point is to have fun and try something new – and maybe a little scary --- rather than to be the "best" singer. Even those who choose not to sing can be there to cheer and support their team mates. And often, people who are resistant to the idea of singing at the beginning of the event get their courage up by the end, after seeing all their colleagues up on stage.

Dinner/Potlucks

Sharing food as a method of bonding is a human universal. While your team may sometimes share lunch and other meals as part of their work, creating social gatherings where the point is to share and enjoy food and not talk about work is an excellent way to encourage team building. You can plan a dinner out, or you can institute regular potluck dinners. Potlucks give people a chance to showcase their cooking, and are more budget-friendly than always going out. Organize potlucks with a theme, and have a sign-up sheet so that people know what's being brought. Be sure to take into account team members with special dietary needs (vegetarian, gluten-free, kosher).

Physical Activities

Another great way to build a team is to engage in physical activities together. This can include competitive sports, such as golf or volleyball. But you can also schedule gatherings around activities just for the sake of engaging in some physical exercise. Activities such as nature walks, ice or roller skating, dancing (including dance lessons), and biking can be even more fun when shared. You might also investigate activities like mini golf and laser tag which, while competitive, are as much about the fun of playing as they are about winning. Keep in mind team members who might have physical differences or challenges, including those who use wheelchairs or other mobility equipment, when creating gatherings focused around physical activity. You can always find activities in which these members of your team can participate, and many venues have specialized equipment or other assistance. When creating a gathering focused around physical activity, encourage everyone to participate. Put the focus on the shared experience and the fun, not on being the best or more proficient at the activity.

Meetings

Meetings aren't exactly at the top of the list when people think of fun social gatherings. However, you can use your regular meetings to help build your team in several ways. Have time to check in with each other. Include lunch or snacks to make the meeting more enjoyable. Encourage people to interact and share during the meeting. Meetings can also be held in places outside the office, whether over a meal or just in a different location, to add some variety. Meetings need not be a burden. And given that you are likely having regular meetings with your team, they are a built-in opportunity for some team building.

Chapter 8 – Common Mistakes When Team Building

Even the most carefully created team building plan may fall prey to mistakes. Because people are all different, what works in one group may be less successful in others. There are some common mistakes that occur when team building. Being aware of these mistakes ahead of time can help you avoid them. And if they do occur, you'll be able to quickly spot them and correct course.

Allowing Cliques to Develop

One of the most common errors when team building is allowing cliques to develop. This happens when a group of people become insular and only want to interact with each other. They may exclude others, gossip, or simply keep themselves apart from the rest of the team. Clearly, this is exactly the opposite of what we want to happen when we are engaging in team building. The other side of cliques developing is that certain people may be consistently left out, ostracized, or otherwise excluded. Be attentive if you see cliques developing. Some signs that cliques are developing may include:

- People only wanting to team or pair with each other

- The same groups or teams consistently forming

- The same person being consistently left out or left until last

You can help avoid clique formation by encouraging (or even requiring) people to team or pair with different team members. Encourage interaction with the whole group. Also make conscious effort to include everyone and invite everyone to participate.

Not Delegating Tasks

A failure to delegate can undermine team building. Be sure to delegate tasks when you facilitate team building. Also make clear that, when working in groups, tasks should be delegated. It is not uncommon for team members who are very focused on "winning" or "being the best" to take over group activities and not delegate to their group members. Reinforce how important this is, and that the goal is not winning at all costs. You might include activities which teach and reinforce delegation skills. When tasks are not delegated, the team does not get the experience of working together – they are simply led by the "expert." This can create resentment and lead to negative feelings and interactions among the team.

Rewarding in Private/Criticizing in Public

Feedback is a key component of team building. A common mistake people make when team building is to only give negative or developmental feedback when with the whole team, while reserving rewards and positive feedback for private times. This is especially egregious if there are one or two team members who are consistently criticized in public but only rewarded in private (or worse, not rewarded at all). Developmental feedback is important, but if a team has a sense that they do nothing right, or that they are going to be called out or humiliated in public, they develop resentment and low morale. Be sure to save individual developmental feedback for private meetings with the person. You can give developmental feedback to the whole team when you are together. And make sure to praise as openly as you offer developmental feedback.

Disjointed Plans of Grandeur

As dangerous as it is not to have a team building plan, having a plan that is too complex or grandiose is also something to avoid. A common mistake when creating a team building plan is to pack the schedule with too many activities, trainings, and meetings. This makes your plan unnecessarily complex. Also be wary of expecting miracles – that one session of broomball or one potluck will solve any interpersonal problems in your team. Keep your team building plan interesting, but avoid making it too ornate, multi-faceted, or complex. Plans like this are frustrating to administer and manage, and even more frustrating for the team members who have to engage in the activities. They may result in resentment of you and the program, which does little to build your team!

Chapter 9 – Formatting a Team Building Plan

Like any other key initiative, team building needs a plan. Take the time to format a solid team building plan so that you know where you're going. This helps you keep your team abreast of what's happening, what they can expect, and what they need to do. Create your team building plan with input from your team, as well as your own research. Create a plan that is manageable and realistic, yet diverse and fun.

Define the Goal

The most important step is to define the goal of your team building plan. Just saying you want to "build a team" isn't enough. What needs to change or improve on your team? This will help you focus your team building efforts. Also take into account the circumstances of your team. Are you spread out over many office locations? How large is your team? What special considerations are there, such as remote employees or heavy travel schedules? Some common goals for team building include:

- Improved interpersonal communication

- Improved collaboration

- Higher morale

- Greater camaraderie

- Integration of new team members into an existing team

- Motivating the team

Based on your goal or goals, choose activities that best support what you are trying to achieve. Be sure to evaluate your plan regularly in case your goals change.

In addition to an overall goal for your team building plan, it is key to define a goal for each team building activity and clearly articulate it.

Consult Team Members

Your team members are your best source of information when you plan team building activities. There is no sense in scheduling social gatherings, for example, that no one comes to! Take the time to ask your team what kind of activities they'd like to engage in and what they would like to do. Also ask them what they think could be improved about your team and how you might go about making those improvements occur. Taking time to consult your team shows that you want to create a team building plan that works for them, and that you are invested in what they care about and have to say. Check in with your team often about different activities. Also encourage your team to come to you when they have new ideas for team building activities.

Research and Create Structure

After you've consulted your team, research their suggestions. Look at what industry leaders and your colleagues are doing in terms of team building. Spend some time surfing the Internet, which is a wealth of team building ideas, as well as looking at books of team building activities and games. Figure out what types of activities are possible and practical for you to do. This may include creating a budget, contacting outside vendors and consultants, and otherwise examining the logistics of various activities. Then create a structure. Decide in what order you will do activities or what goals you will address first. Determine whether you'll have monthly, bimonthly, or more/less frequent team building activities. If possible, start putting these on a calendar. Then communicate with your team what this schedule will be like. Let them know what to expect. Having a structure in place helps make it easier to consistently implement your team building activities and plans.

Keep It Fun

Perhaps the most important thing when creating a team building plan is to keep it fun! If team building is a drudgery, your team is not likely to benefit from it. Find ways to keep even meetings and trainings infused with a sense of fun. Balance more task-oriented sessions with fun activities. Have a sense of play. Make note as you research of ideas for infusing team building with levity and fun. This will help ensure that your team gets the greatest benefit from your plan. And don't be afraid to revise your plan if you start to implement is and realize that no one's having any fun!

Chapter 10 – Evaluate

Always take time to evaluate your team building efforts. This way you know what works well and what can be changed or gotten rid of. There are some steps you should take after each team building activity, and then at the end of the year or period to evaluate the entire team building plan. Be sure to take these steps so that you can make your team building efforts the best they can be. Never be afraid to switch things up or alter your team building to better suit your team's needs. The goal is always to best serve what the team and the organization need.

Was the Goal Met?

After each team building exercise, ask whether the goal was met. You can ascertain this by handing out evaluation forms or seeking other feedback from participants. You can also watch over the following days to see if any related changes take place. If the goal was met, you know that the team building activity or exercise was a quality one. If you find that the goal was not met, it is important to evaluate why. It may not mean that the activity itself was inherently poor, but that other factors might have interfered with its effectiveness. Take time to honestly evaluate each team building activity. Also take time to evaluate the whole plan at the end of the year, quarter, or other logical time period.

Was the Team Building Cohesive?

Also ask yourself if the team building was cohesive. Did it flow logically? Did the different parts of it make sense? Did the team understand the goal of the team building activity? Again, seeking feedback from your team is one excellent way to help determine this. Also reflect on your own observations or participation in the activity. Was there a piece that seemed out of place? What worked? What didn't? Reflect on any incoherencies and address them in other team development activities. Also be sure to evaluate the entire team building plan to see if it is cohesive, with all the parts supporting each other.

What Did the Team Think of the Team Building?

Ask your team what they thought of the team building. Did they enjoy it? Did they find it helpful? Would they like to the same or similar activities in the future? If they did enjoy the team building, ask them specifically what they enjoyed or appreciated. This will help you choose future activities. By the same token, if your team did not enjoy a team building, ask them what they disliked. This will give you valuable data on what works and does not work for your team. When you find activities that your team enjoys, find ways to offer the same or similar types of team building in the future.

How Can the Team Building Be Improved for Next Time?

Keep a continuous improvement mindset when it comes to team building. What can you do differently to improve the team building next time? Even successful team building activities may have room for improvement. Feedback from the team comes in here. If the team didn't enjoy a team building, ask them what you could do differently next time. If you discover that a team building did not achieve its goal, work to determine why it failed, so that you can improve it the next time. Seek out areas where the team building is not cohesive or seems to break down, and see if you can improve it and future team buildings.

Additional Titles

The 90 Minute Guide series of books covers a variety of general business skills and are intended to be completed in 90 minutes or less. It is an effective way for building your skill set and can be used to acquire professional development units needed by project managers and other industries to maintain their certification. For the availability of titles please see

https://www.silvercitypublications.com/shop/.

No. 1 - Appreciative Inquiry

No. 2 - Assertiveness and Self Control

No. 3 - Attention Management

No. 4 - Body Language Basics

No. 5 - Business Acumen

No. 6 - Business and Etiquette

No. 7 - Change Management

No. 8 - Coaching and Mentoring

No. 9 - Communications Strategies

No. 10 - Conflict Resolution

No. 34 - Team Building for Management

No. 35 - Team Work and Team Building

No. 36 - Time Management

No. 37 - Top 10 Soft Skills You Need

No. 38 - Virtual Team Building and Management

www.ingramcontent.com/pod-product-compliance
Lightning Source LLC
Chambersburg PA
CBHW070723210326
41520CB00016B/4436